Latin Americans Thought of It

Latin Americans Thought of It

AMAZING INNOVATIONS

Eva Salinas

annick press
toronto + new york + vancouver

© 2012 Eva Salinas (text)
Cover and interior design by Sheryl Shapiro
Edited by David MacDonald
Maps on pages 10–11 and running figure on page 19 by Tina Holdcroft

A sincere thank-you to expert reader Matthew Restall, Edwin Erle Sparks Professor of Latin American History at Pennsylvania State University, University Park, Pennsylvania.

Annick Press Ltd.
All rights reserved. No part of this work covered by the copyrights hereon may be reproduced or used in any form or by any means—graphic, electronic, or mechanical—without the prior written permission of the publisher.

We acknowledge the support of the Canada Council for the Arts, the Ontario Arts Council, and the Government of Canada through the Canada Book Fund (CBF) for our publishing activities.

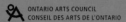 ONTARIO ARTS COUNCIL
CONSEIL DES ARTS DE L'ONTARIO

Cataloging in Publication

Salinas, Eva
    Latin Americans thought of it : amazing innovations / Eva Salinas.

(We thought of it)
Includes index.
Issued also in Spanish under title: Lo inventaron los latinoamericanos.
ISBN 978-1-55451-376-5 (pbk.).—ISBN 978-1-55451-377-2 (bound)

    1. Inventions—Latin America—History—Juvenile literature.
2. Latin America—Intellectual life—Juvenile literature. 3. Latin America—Civilization—Juvenile literature.
I. Title. II. Series: We thought of it

T24.A1S25 2012   j609.8   C2011-907327-7

Distributed in Canada by:
Firefly Books Ltd.
66 Leek Crescent
Richmond Hill, ON
L4B 1H1

Published in the U.S.A. by:
Annick Press (U.S.) Ltd.
Distributed in the U.S.A. by:
Firefly Books (U.S.) Inc.
P.O. Box 1338
Ellicott Station
Buffalo, NY 14205

Watch for more books in the We Thought of It series, coming soon.

Printed in China.

Visit us at: www.annickpress.com

For my family in Canada—Joan, Jim, and Luke. Thanks for your love and support. And for my Chileno, Christian.
—E.S.

Contents

WELCOME/ 6

MAPS/ 10

CLOTHING/ 12

WORKING THE LAND/ 14

ARCHITECTURE/ 16

COMMUNICATION/ 18

ARTS AND CRAFTS/ 20

EVERYDAY INVENTIONS/ 24

FOOD AND DRINK/ 26

CELEBRATIONS/ 30

MUSIC AND DANCE/ 32

SPORTS/ 36

LATIN AMERICA TODAY/ 38

TIMELINE/ 42

FURTHER READING/ 43

INDEX/ 45

Bienvenido, Bem-vindo,

Eva in the fishing town of Lota, Chile

My Journey

Saludos amigos! My name is Eva. I was born in Canada, to a South American father and a Canadian mother. I spent many years imagining the place where my father and his family came from. Finally, one day I decided to move there to connect with my roots.

I remember my first visit to Latin America. Our airplane flew all night over great stretches of land and water, over jungle, desert, and enormous mountains that reached up into the sky. I landed in Chile, where my father was born and raised before he moved to North America—as many Latin Americans have done, bringing their culture and history with them.

While living in Chile, I discovered that its capital city, Santiago, is full of life and very busy. Like many big cities in North America, it has tall office buildings, beautiful parks, and subways. I experienced the culture of Chile in many different ways—eating seafood by the ocean with my uncle, listening to Andean folk musicians and Mapuche drummers, gathering with friends and relatives to eat the traditional small evening meal called *once* (pronounced *own-say*), and dancing the cueca during Chile's Independence Day celebrations.

Welcome.

Thanks to my father, I was born with Chile in my blood. Now, after having spent much time there, it is part of my soul.

What Is Latin America?

Latin America is a relatively new term, only a few hundred years old. But the story of its people is much older.

Chile's busy capital city, Santiago

The Andes Mountains, seen from an airplane

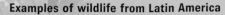

Examples of wildlife from Latin America

When Christopher Columbus sailed to the Caribbean Islands and, on a later voyage, Central America, Europeans thought he had discovered a "new world." At that time, they did not know about the Caribbean Islands and the American continent. But this "world" wasn't new at all—it had been home to many different cultures for thousands of years.

Latin America is not a continent. It is a large region with about 20 countries spread across North, Central, and South America, as well as in the Caribbean. People use the terms *Latin America* and *Latin Americans* as a means of acknowledging the cultural similarities among the people who live in these countries. One important similarity is that most of the people in these countries speak Spanish, although in Brazil—the largest country in South America—most people speak Portuguese.

There are some countries south of the United States that are not usually considered part of Latin America (for example, Belize, Suriname, and Guyana). People in these countries have closer ties to cultures from Africa or Europe (other than Spain or Portugal).

Many people who live in Latin America don't often call themselves Latin Americans. They prefer to think of themselves as proud citizens of their own country— for example, as Mexicans, Cubans, or Bolivians.

An illustration from an Aztec book

Your Journey

This book is a celebration of the achievements and innovations of Latin American cultures. From the ancient peoples of the past to the people of today, Latin Americans have created amazing innovations—Mayan pyramids, new ways of farming, and lively music and dance styles, just to name a few. Some of these innovations are well known, while others may be new to you. There are many more that I was not able to include, but this book is a good place to start your journey of discovery. It has certainly been a fascinating journey for me, and I hope it will be just as enjoyable for you.

Young people in Panama compete in a motocross race.

Colombian singer and songwriter Shakira

MAPS OF LATIN AMERICA

Mexico

Cuba

Haiti*

Dominican Republic

Belize*

Honduras

Puerto Rico†

Guatemala

El Salvador

Nicaragua

Costa Rica

Venezuela

Panama

Guyana*

Suriname*

Colombia

French Guyana*

Ecuador

Peru

Bolivia

Brazil

Paraguay

Chile

Argentina

Uruguay

★ The cultures in these countries are not generally considered primarily Latin American.

† Puerto Rico is a U.S. territory, but the culture is Latin American.

Sonora Desert

Chihuahuan Desert

Lake Chapala

Lake Nicaragua

Orinoco River

Amazon Rainforest

Amazon River

Andes Mountains

Lake Titicaca

Atacama Desert

Parana River

Patagonian Desert*

* The Patagonian Desert is not a typical sandy desert. Some areas are rocky, while others are covered with grass or shrubs.

CLOTHING

Some clothing items from Latin America have become symbols of national pride. Others have become fashion items that are now worn around the world.

The Kuna people of Panama make colorful fabric art to use in blouses.

Sombrero

The word *sombrero* comes from the Spanish word *sombra*, meaning "shade." In the Spanish-speaking world, a sombrero is any kind of hat with a brim that provides shade from the sun.

After the Spanish brought a brimmed hat to Latin America, the Mexicans developed their own unique version—a sombrero made of straw or felt, with a wide brim, a tapered top, and a chin strap. Some sombreros have intricate, embroidered designs. Traditionally worn by ranchers, the Mexican sombrero is now famous around the world.

Mexicans often wear sombreros at parades and festivals.

Former U.S. president Harry Truman wears a Panama hat in the 1940s.

Panama Hat

This light-colored hat actually comes from Ecuador, where it is called *sombrero de paja toquilla* (Spanish for "straw hat of the toquilla plant"). The Panama hat's brim protected workers' ears and neck from the sun. The Spanish brought this style of hat back to Europe, where it became very popular in the 1700s CE. The Panama hat gained worldwide popularity in 1906, when U.S. president Theodore Roosevelt was photographed wearing one while on a visit to Panama. Back then, this hat was shipped from Panama, which is how it got its name.

Clockwise from far left: alpaca, vicuña, guanaco, and llama

Wool

The winter season in the Andes Mountains of South America can get very cold. The people who live there are lucky that the mountains are also home to four animals—the alpaca, vicuña, guanaco, and llama—whose fur provides wool to make warm clothing. These animals are related to the Arabian camel, but have more fur and can survive in very cold and high habitats.

Alpacas have fine, light wool, which is preferred for most clothing. The wool of the vicuña is silky yet warm, and in ancient times was reserved for Inca royalty. Today, the vicuña is a protected species and is the national animal of Peru.

A Guatemalan woman wears a huipil while using a backstrap loom.

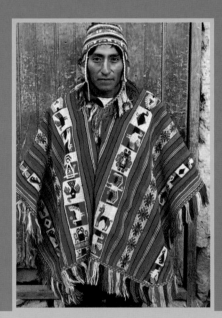

A traditional poncho from Peru

Poncho

The Mapuche people of Chile and Argentina live in the most southern part of the Andes Mountains, where the weather is often cold and rainy. Hundreds of years ago, the Mapuche created a unique garment to help them stay warm—they made a slit in a heavy woolen blanket (to allow the head to pass through) and wore it over their shoulders. This garment, called a poncho, allowed people's arms to move freely.

Today, ponchos are worn throughout Latin America and around the world. There are even modern plastic ponchos that protect people from rain.

Huipil

The huipil (pronounced *wee-peel*) is the traditional blouse worn by women in Central America, mainly Guatemala, Belize, and El Salvador. The cloth is woven on a portable loom called a backstrap loom.

Traditionally, the colorful design on the blouse would tell something about the woman wearing it— usually which community she was from. Some of the patterns can be traced back to Mayan designs over 1000 years old. Today, women in Central America still take great pride in weaving the huipil.

WORKING THE LAND

From ancient times until the present day, Latin Americans have been creative in using the land around them to help make their communities bigger and stronger.

Irrigation

Irrigation (the process of watering farmland) has been used in Latin America for thousands of years, from Mexico to South America. The largest ancient irrigation system was built in northern Peru, where people lived in the mountains.

Most of the rain falls near the tops of mountains, leaving valleys and lower areas dry. To solve this problem, the Incas built long stone canals that captured water and carried it to valleys, villages, and farms. This irrigation system made it easier to grow crops and feed a larger number of people. Irrigation also meant that farmers did not have to wait for rain to fall on their fields, so the crops grew more quickly and could be harvested before the first frosts came and killed the plants.

Many canals were built beside roads, and these canals provided traveling people and their llamas with drinking water. Some irrigation canals built in the 1500s CE still exist and are being restored so they can be used again.

A stone canal originally built by the Incas

Raised Fields

Raised fields were human-made islands created in long strips in a lake or swampy areas. To make each island, people built walls using reeds and wooden posts. The space inside the walls was filled with layers of dead plants and mud, and crops were planted on top. This method of farming was used in Mexico, Central America, and Bolivia.

The earliest known raised fields were created about 700 years ago, or perhaps even earlier. The raised fields in Mexico (called *chinampas*) are famous because they made it possible for the Aztecs to feed the growing city of Tenochtitlan, now called Mexico City. Today, chinampas can still be seen in the Xochimilco area of Mexico City, where they are most often used to grow flowers.

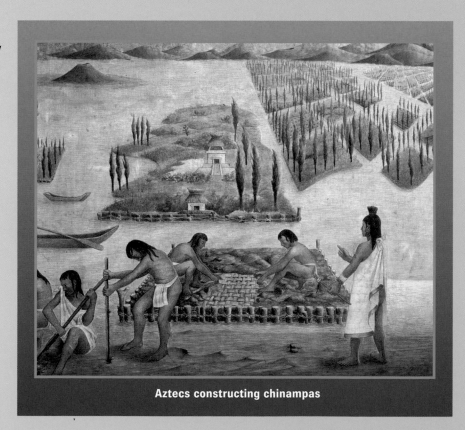

Aztecs constructing chinampas

Terraces used for farming at
Machu Picchu (see page 16)

Mountain Farming

For the people who lived in the mountainous
Andes region of South America, farming was
a challenge. The mountainsides received
more sunlight than the valleys, but it was
difficult to grow crops on sloping land.

Farmers overcame this problem by
creating fields that rose like steps up
a mountainside. These steps (called
terraces) were made using stone, soil,
and fertilizer. The terraces provided flat land
for crops to grow and made it easier for the
land to absorb rainwater. Terraces also
prevented erosion.

Different crops grew well at different
places on the mountainside. Families traded
crops with each other, which gave people
more variety in their diet.

Labor Tax

Today, citizens in most countries
pay taxes to the government in
return for services such as
schooling and road-building.
The Incas in Peru used a similar
system to build their great
empire, but instead of paying the
government tax money, citizens
provided labor. This was called
the *mit'a* system. For a period
of time each year, the head of
each family would work for the
government. Some people
worked in mines, digging for
gold, silver, or useful minerals,
while others built roads or
served in the army.

Inset: Modern miners in Bolivia
Background: These salt mines in
Peru were first used by the Incas.

ARCHITECTURE

In some Latin American cultures, expert builders used innovative techniques to create amazing structures—some of which still stand today.

Machu Picchu

Machu Picchu is a small Inca city, built around 1450 CE, that sits high in the Andes Mountains of Peru. The location of the city suggests that it was meant to be a secret. It is not visible from the valleys below, and the Spanish never discovered it when they arrived in the 1500s.

After an American professor came across Machu Picchu in 1911, people wondered about the purpose of this "secret city." Today, some experts believe that it was a quiet place where Inca royalty could get away from the noise of the city, and it was also home to a religious community.

Machu Picchu shows us some of the Inca's remarkable achievements in building techniques and engineering. The city had nearly 200 stone buildings; waterways that channeled rainwater for drinking, bathing, and growing crops; and more than a dozen water fountains. Another interesting fact about Machu Picchu is that the Incas had not discovered the wheel, so they did not use wheeled carts to transport building materials. Yet they were still able to create this amazing city at the top of a mountain.

A waterway carved in stone at Machu Picchu

A view of Machu Picchu as it appears today

For information on terrace farming, a technique used at Machu Picchu, see page 15.

A stone wall built by the Incas

Building for Earthquakes

Along the Pacific coast of Latin America, earthquakes are common. Throughout the ages, some communities constructed buildings in a way that would prevent or minimize earthquake damage. Inca stonework is one of the best examples.

The Incas cut granite blocks into irregular shapes and then fitted the blocks tightly together, like puzzle pieces. Walls were built with an inward slant and rounded corners. These techniques helped stone structures, including some at Machu Picchu, last for hundreds of years and survive many earthquakes.

Today, some countries around the world—including Chile—have strict rules for building structures in a way that makes them strong enough to withstand earthquakes.

A Mayan pyramid in Guatemala

Mayan Pyramids

More than 2000 years ago, the ancient Maya built large cities in the jungles of Mexico, Guatemala, and some parts of Belize, Honduras, and El Salvador. These cities often included several limestone pyramids that were built to honor the gods. Today, these pyramids are considered architectural wonders.

The Mayan style of pyramid is unique, with differences that set it apart from the most famous Egyptian pyramids. The Egyptian pyramids originally had smooth sides and a pointed tip at the top. Mayan pyramids have sides built like huge steps. At the top there is a temple, often with a flat roof. Usually two or four sets of steep stairs lead up to the temple. Along with their religious purpose, Mayan pyramids served as landmarks for travelers because the pyramids were visible above the surrounding jungle.

COMMUNICATION

Some ancient societies in Latin America developed unique ways of recording and communicating information, including hieroglyphs and complex calendar systems.

Mayan hieroglyphs

Mayan Hieroglyphs

The Maya developed a system of writing that used pictures and symbols called hieroglyphs. (The ancient Egyptians also wrote using hieroglyphs, but they used different pictures and symbols to write in their own language.) The Maya used hieroglyphs to record the history of their culture, including stories about important events, their kings, and their religious beliefs.

The Maya wrote the first hieroglyphs as early as 400 BCE. When the Spanish arrived in Central America in the 1500s CE, they ordered hundreds of Mayan books to be destroyed. A few books survived, along with writing on pottery, walls, and stone monuments.

Experts tried for many years to interpret Mayan hieroglyphs, with limited success. But an American researcher named David Stuart made important discoveries about the language in the 1980s. These discoveries allowed experts to better understand Mayan writing and learn more about Mayan history.

Today, some communities in Central America are learning for the first time how to read the hieroglyphs, so they can connect with the culture and history of their ancestors.

Calendar Systems

Many ancient cultures of Mexico and Central America created calendar systems to keep track of time and dates. Early calendar systems from this region may have been created as long ago as 500 BCE.

Like the calendar we use today, many ancient Latin American calendars were based on the solar system. (In our modern calendar, a year is the time it takes the Earth to orbit once around the Sun.) Because the Maya were very interested in studying the stars and planets, it is not surprising that the Mayan calendar— developed more than 2000 years ago— was one of the most accurate calendar systems of ancient times.

The Aztecs also had a calendar system, which is very similar to the Mayan calendar.

The Aztec "Sun Stone" describes how the Aztecs measured time.

Quipu

Ancient peoples living in the Andes Mountains of South America did not have a writing system, but they developed the quipu (pronounced *kee-poo*; sometimes spelled *khipu*) as a way to record information.

A quipu was made with anywhere from a few to more than a thousand cotton or wool cords, which were dyed different colors and attached to a main cord. To record information, people tied knots into the cords. By using different styles and combinations of knots, along with the different colors of cords, people were able to record a wide variety of messages.

The Incas adopted the quipu from their ancestors and used it to record information about such things as community populations, warehouse supplies, flocks of animals, and military groups.

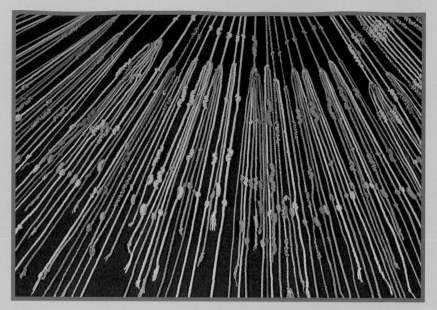

The original colors have faded from this Inca quipu.

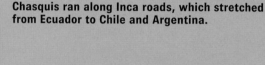

Chasquis ran along Inca roads, which stretched from Ecuador to Chile and Argentina.

Inca Messengers

When the Incas wanted to send a message or a gift for royalty over a long distance, they used messengers called *chasquis* (pronounced *chass-kees*; sometimes spelled *chaskis*). A chasqui could run very quickly. He carried the message or goods along an Inca road until he reached a cabin called a *tambo*, where more chasquis waited. Then a different chasqui would carry the message or goods for a distance, until reaching the next tambo. This system was similar to modern relay races and allowed important messages to travel quickly—about 240 kilometers (150 miles) per day.

A chasqui holds a quipu and blows a shell horn to let people know he is coming.

ARTS AND CRAFTS

From murals to masks to decorated eggs, Latin American arts and crafts are famous for their bright colors and distinctive designs.

Mayan Murals

A mural is a work of art painted on a wall. Talented Mayan artists painted large murals inside buildings and caves. Many of these murals tell the history of the Mayan people by showing kings and important events such as battles. Some of the murals are over 2000 years old.

Mayan artists used minerals and vegetables to create paints in a variety of colors. Unfortunately, most of their murals have not survived because the colors faded away over centuries in the hot, humid climate of the Mayan jungle.

Some of the most famous Mayan murals can be seen at Bonampak, Mexico. There, a long building has three rooms covered with murals showing such things as a ceremony with dancers, musicians playing instruments, and prisoners captured during war.

A mural from Bonampak, Mexico

Gourd Carving

Several different regions in Latin America have been home to expert gourd carvers for hundreds—even thousands—of years.

In Peru, artists use a sharp tool to carve scenes of daily life into the gourd. In some villages, the gourd is lightly burned and the design is carved into the darkened areas. In other villages, the gourd is sometimes colored with dyes and then carved. Some ancient carvers pressed objects such as pieces of shell into the gourd to complete the design. Gourds were often used as plates or bowls.

Some Guatemalan artists use a special technique to prepare gourds for carving. First, the gourd is dried out and polished, and then it is rubbed with lacquer to give it a glossy coating. Next, it is dyed with a mix of tree ash and grease. Then the gourd is ready for carving.

A carved gourd from an artist of the Quechua people of Peru

A scene from a Diego Rivera mural celebrating the history of Mexico

Modern Mexican Murals

In the 1920s, artists in Mexico began to create public murals. These murals were painted on the outside of buildings such as schools and government offices. The artists who created the murals believed that art should be free so that everyone could enjoy it. They also believed that art could communicate an important story or message.

Many public murals celebrate Mexican culture, especially its connection to the Aztecs. Other murals show the lives of everyday people and the struggles they faced. Diego Rivera is the most famous painter of Mexican murals. His art, along with the murals of other Mexican painters, has influenced artists around the world.

Metal Work

During ancient times, the Incas and other cultures from the Andes region created beautiful objects from metal.

A beautiful example of Inca gold work

The Incas often worked with gold and silver because for them gold represented the Sun and silver represented the Moon. To get these precious metals from pieces of rock, Inca miners sometimes created special clay furnaces with holes in them. Wind blew in through the holes, providing oxygen that made the fire hot enough to melt the metal in the rock. The Incas used the metal to create a variety of objects, including gold plates, silver or gold figurines of people and animals, and silver drinking cups for Inca royalty.

Very few gold and silver objects from the Incas exist today. Many were seized by Spanish explorers and melted down to create gold bars and coins so the valuable metals would be easy to transport back to Spain.

ARTS AND CRAFTS *continued*

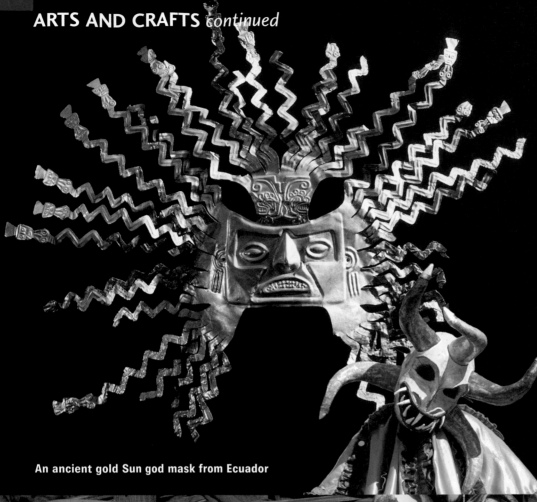

An ancient gold Sun god mask from Ecuador

Masks

Some of the world's most fascinating masks were made by ancient cultures in Latin America. Thousands of years ago, the Olmec people made masks out of jade, a stone that is often green in color. Other ancient cultures often made masks out of gold, sometimes representing the Sun god. More recent masks made in Ecuador feature bright colors and show animal faces, such as a monkey, dog, or pig.

Many cultures in Latin America still make beautiful and unusual masks, most often for festivals such as Carnival (see page 31).

A Carnival mask from Puerto Rico

Cascarones

Brightly decorated eggs are familiar to people who celebrate Easter. In Mexico there is a special kind of egg called a *cascarón*, which people make to celebrate Easter, birthdays, and other special days throughout the year.

First, a small hole is made in the eggshell to drain out the contents. Next, the egg is filled with confetti and the shell is painted with one or more bright colors. The best part is saved for last—the egg is broken over someone's head and the confetti spills out. Some people believe that having a cascarón broken over your head will bring good luck.

The very first cascarones were probably made in China, where the eggs were filled with perfumed powder. It was Mexicans who came up with the idea of filling the eggs with confetti. This fun tradition has become popular in other countries, especially in some parts of the United States.

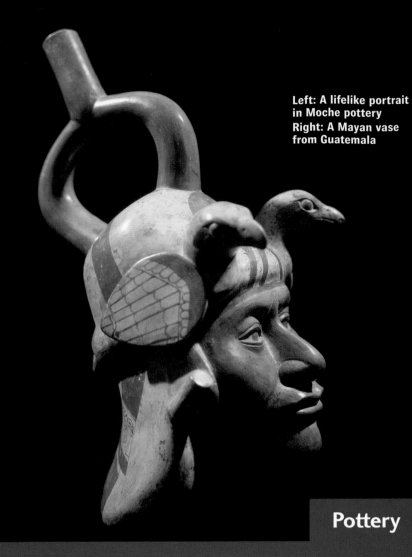

Left: A lifelike portrait in Moche pottery
Right: A Mayan vase from Guatemala

Pottery

For thousands of years, Latin American artists from Mexico to Honduras to Ecuador have created clay pottery with unique and interesting designs. Some of the oldest pottery has been found in Brazil and may have been created 7000 years ago.

About 1500 years ago, the Maya were creating a variety of objects from clay, including cups, vases, and incense burners. They often decorated their pottery with scenes from their history, as they did on their murals. At about the same time,

the Moche people in northern Peru used clay to craft cups and other useful items in the shape of three-dimensional portraits of real people.

Later, the Inca in Peru created bowls and jugs that were baked at a high temperature and then carefully polished. The designs on this pottery include lines, triangles, and squares.

Today, many Latin American countries continue to produce pottery that is admired around the world.

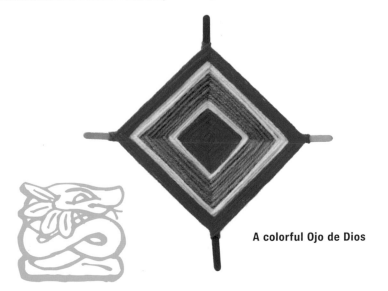

A colorful Ojo de Dios

Ojo de Dios

An Ojo de Dios (pronounced *oh-ho day dee-ose*; Spanish for "eye of God") is made by weaving colorful yarn around two crossed sticks to make a diamond shape. This craft, which was developed by the Huichol people of Mexico, originally had a religious meaning—it represented the eye of God watching over the people.

In Mexico there is a tradition that a father will make an Ojo de Dios for each of his children. The central portion is woven when the child is born. Another section is added each year until the child is five years old.

EVERYDAY INVENTIONS

Many different kinds of plants grow throughout Latin America. People used these plants to make a variety of things—some useful in everyday life, and some just for fun.

Chewing Gum

Chewing gum was once made by boiling chicle, the sticky sap of the sapodilla tree. This tree grows in various places in Latin America, especially the tropical regions of Central America.

The Maya have been chewing on chicle for hundreds of years—possibly even longer—and they used it to help ease hunger or thirst. The Aztecs in Mexico also chewed it, sometimes to cure bad breath, but it wasn't considered polite to chew in public.

In the mid-1800s CE, the Mexican General Antonio Lopez de Santa Anna brought chicle to the United States. Today, most chewing gum is no longer made from chicle, so very few *chicleros* (the farmers who harvest the sap) remain in Central America.

A Mexican chiclero harvests chicle.

Hammock

Most experts believe that the hammock was first used in the Caribbean Islands and Central America about 1000 years ago. The first hammocks were made from tree bark, although plant leaves, palm branches, and eventually cotton were later used. A hammock was a good place to sleep because it was raised above the ground, so it offered protection from dangerous insects and animals such as snakes.

In the late 1400s CE, some of the first Spanish explorers to arrive at the Caribbean Islands found the native Taíno people sleeping in hammocks. These explorers decided to use hammocks for sleeping while at sea, and they introduced this invention to Europe when they returned home. Today, hammocks are popular around the world.

A modern hammock

Tobacco

The tobacco plant has been growing throughout Latin America for perhaps as long as thousands of years. When Christopher Columbus and his crew arrived in Cuba in 1492 CE, they found people smoking large rolls of dried tobacco leaves—similar to what we now call a cigar. Columbus's men picked up the habit and it spread around the world. As early as the 1600s, people began to realize that smoking tobacco was very bad for your health and also highly addictive.

A Cuban man rolls cigars by hand.

Worry Dolls

In Guatemala, there is a legend parents tell children to help them sleep at night: If children tell their worries to a set of tiny dolls made from scraps of material and tuck the dolls under their pillow, by morning their worries will be gone. Today, these "worry dolls" are still popular with children, and many tourists buy them as souvenirs.

Latex flowing from a rubber tree in Brazil

Rubber

About 3500 years ago, the Olmec people of Central America discovered how to make rubber. They collected the sap (called latex) of the Panama rubber tree, mixed it with juice from a vine that grew in the region, and then heated the mixture. (*Olmec* means "people of the rubber land" in the Aztec language.)

The Olmecs used rubber to make such things as sandals with rubber soles, elastic bands, and rubber balls. The rubber balls were used to play a ceremonial game that took place on a stone-lined court. Some people believe that modern ball games such as soccer are based on the ancient Olmec game.

A modern rubber shoe sole

FOOD AND DRINK

Did you know that some of the world's most popular foods originally came from Latin America? Tasty and nutritious foods from Latin American cultures can now be found on dinner tables around the world.

Curanto

Above: Uncovering the curanto
Right: The curanto is ready to eat.

Curanto is a traditional dish that comes from the island of Chiloé in southern Chile. The ingredients are usually seafood, meat, potatoes, and vegetables, which are cooked in a special way. Rocks are heated in a fire until they are extremely hot. Then they are placed in a hole in the ground and the food is put on top of the rocks. Next, everything is covered with leaves to hold in the heat. Once the food is cooked, it is uncovered and the feast begins.

In the language of the Mapuche people, *curanto* means "hot stones." Curanto is still very popular in southern Chile and is often prepared for large gatherings and celebrations.

Freeze-Dried Food

More than 600 years ago—centuries before astronauts took freeze-dried snacks into space—people who lived in the grasslands of the Andes Mountains freeze-dried food to preserve it. First, they left the food outside during cold nights so it would freeze. During the day, the food would dry out in the sun. Then people stomped on the food to squeeze out any moisture that remained. The process took several days to complete, and made food last much longer without spoiling.

In the Andes, people used this process most often for potatoes, though they also freeze-dried meat. Because freeze-dried food was lighter yet still very nutritious, it was ideal for travelers or soldiers to carry on long journeys.

Modern freeze-dried food prepared for astronauts

Chocolate

Chocolate is made from the seeds, or "beans," of the cacao (pronounced *kuh-kay-oh* or *kuh-kow*) tree, which first grew in tropical areas of South and Central America. As early as 1500 BCE, the Olmec people of southern Mexico became one of the first to use cacao beans as food. The Maya and later the Aztecs also used cacao, mixing ground beans with water to make a chocolate drink. This drink was bitter rather than sweet, and was a luxury only the wealthiest people could afford. Cacao beans were so valuable that they were also used as money.

In the 1500s CE, Spanish explorers brought cacao beans back to Spain. The Spanish added vanilla and sugar to make a sweeter version of the Aztec drink. By the 1600s, chocolate was being used in cakes and desserts. The first chocolate bar was created in England in the 1800s.

Cacao trees now grow in many countries, and Brazil is one of the top producers of cacao beans.

Cacao pods grow on a cacao tree.

Cacao "beans" are the seeds found inside the pods.

Champurrado is a thick hot chocolate drink popular in Mexico.

What is the difference between cacao and cocoa (pronounced *ko-ko*)?

Experts disagree on the answer to this question. The tree is always called a cacao tree, but some people call the beans cocoa beans rather than cacao beans. The powder made from just the beans and the powder sold in stores are often called cocoa powder. It's quite possible that the word *cocoa* was created when someone misspelled *cacao*.

FOOD AND DRINK *continued*

Chili Peppers

Chili peppers first grew in Latin America, where farmers have been growing them for thousands of years. Now popular around the world, chili peppers are an important ingredient in many traditional Latin American dishes. There are lots of different types of chili pepper. Some are spicy or "hot," while others are sweet. Here are just a few:

Type		Color	Originally From	How Hot?
Bell		Many colors, including red, green, and yellow	Central and South America	Not hot (sweet)
Jalapeño (pronounced *hah-la-pehn-yo*)		Green	Mexico	Medium hot
Aji (pronounced *a-hee*)		Yellow and orange	Peru and Bolivia	Very hot
Tabasco		Red	Mexico	Extremely hot

Mate

Hundreds of years ago, the Guarani people in Paraguay were the first to prepare mate (pronounced *mah-tay*), a hot drink made from the leaves from the yerba mate plant. This drink became popular throughout the region, even among European settlers. Like tea and coffee, mate contains caffeine, which gives an energy boost. Many people believe that mate helps digestion.

Mate has become popular in various places around the world, and it is still a favorite drink in Argentina, Uruguay, and Paraguay, as well as some parts of Brazil, Chile, and Bolivia.

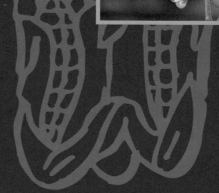
Mate is traditionally served in a gourd cup with a metal straw.

Tomatoes

Tomatoes originally came from the Andes region of South America. Over time, people began to grow tomatoes in Central America and Mexico, where the Spanish saw them for the first time about 500 years ago. The English word *tomato* comes from the Aztec word *tomatl*.

Tomatoes are an important ingredient in recipes from cultures around the world. Many North Americans enjoy tomatoes in salsa, a traditional and often spicy Latin American food served as a dip or a sauce.

Dulce de Leche

It is hard to know where in Latin America this caramel-like sauce was invented because it has been a popular food in many different countries. *Dulce de leche* (pronounced *dool-say day leh-chay*) means "sweet milk" in Spanish. It is made by slowly heating sweetened milk until it becomes thick and light brown in color.

In Latin American countries, dulce de leche is traditionally used in cakes and cookies. In the Dominican Republic and Cuba, it is often flavored with lemon and vanilla or cinnamon, and is served as a pudding.

Many people throughout North America have recently discovered this sweet treat, which is now available in cookies, as an ice cream flavor, and as a flavoring for coffee.

Maize

There was a time when Latin America was the only place to find maize, also known as corn. Some experts say that farmers first began to grow it more than 5000 years ago in Mexico.

Maize was already an important food in Latin America when the Spanish arrived. They took maize back to Spain and soon farmers across Europe were growing it. Eventually, maize became an important crop around the world. It provides food for farm animals as well as humans, and it grows well in many different places.

Maize kernels are ground into a flour that is used to make many popular Latin American foods, such as tortillas, tamales, and corn chips.

A woman prepares corn tortillas.

Potatoes, peanuts, and vanilla beans (used to create vanilla flavoring) first grew in Latin America. Purple potatoes come from Peru.

CELEBRATIONS

Latin Americans love to celebrate many aspects of life with their family and friends. Here are some of the most well-known celebration traditions in Latin America.

A girl tries to break open a traditional piñata.

Piñata

A piñata (pronounced *pin-yah-ta*) is a colorful decoration made from cardboard, papier-mâché, or clay and filled with candies or small toys. The piñata is hung from a string, and a person wearing a blindfold swings a stick to try to break open the piñata to release the treasures inside. In Latin America, piñatas are a favorite part of Christmas and birthday celebrations.

Some experts believe that the idea for the piñata came from a New Year's tradition in China—to bring good luck for the coming year, people would break open clay pots shaped like animals and filled with seeds. When the Europeans arrived in Mexico, they found the Aztecs had their own version of this tradition. On a pole they placed a clay pot, decorated and filled with goodies. Then they broke it open with a stick as a religious offering. The Maya had a similar ritual, but they covered their eyes when aiming at the clay pot, which usually hung on a string.

Day of the Dead

Day of the Dead (called *Dia de los Muertos* in Spanish) is a combination of the Catholic holiday All Saints' Day and a tradition that began thousands of years ago in Latin America. On November 1 and 2, from Mexico to Brazil, people celebrate the lives of those who have died over the past year. The tradition involves visiting a cemetery and placing candles, fake skulls, and flowers (especially marigolds) on the graves of loved ones. Some people also paint their faces to look like skulls. A delicious feast may be prepared, with some of the food set aside to be left at graves.

Food and fake skulls are part of Day of the Dead celebrations.

Carnival celebrations draw large crowds.

Carnival

For many people, the word *carnival* describes any event full of celebration and fun. But in many places around the world, Carnival is a festival that takes place before the Christian holiday period called Lent. Latin American countries celebrate Carnival in their own unique ways. In Brazil, and especially in the city Rio de Janeiro, Carnival is famous for parades with huge, imaginative floats and dancers in colorful costumes.

Quinceañera

In several countries throughout Latin America—especially in Mexico, Cuba, and Puerto Rico—a girl's fifteenth birthday is considered special because it marks the time when a girl becomes a young woman. This important birthday is known as *quinceañera* (Spanish for "fifteen years") or *fiesta de quince años* ("celebration of fifteen years"). Some families mark the day with a church ceremony, while others throw a big party with lots of food.

Dia de la Raza

October 12 (or the Monday nearest to this date) is known in North America as Columbus Day—the day Christopher Columbus arrived in the Americas in 1492. Latin American countries from Mexico to Chile call this day *Dia de la Raza* (Spanish for "Day of the Race"—meaning a day for Latin American people) and take the opportunity to celebrate the rich heritage of their culture.

Girls often wear a fancy dress for their quinceañera.

MUSIC AND DANCE

Many lively styles of music and dance were created in Latin America and are now enjoyed around the world. Latin Americans also developed several unique musical instruments.

Tango

Tango is one of the most famous dances to come from Latin America. In the poorer areas of Buenos Aires (the capital city of Argentina), people first danced the tango in the late 1800s CE. Soon people were also dancing the tango in the neighboring country of Uruguay. When Latin American tango dancers began to perform in Europe in the early 1900s, many people fell in love with this dramatic dance. Soon its popularity spread to the United States.

Tango is also the name of the style of music played for the dance. Tango music is often performed by a six-piece orchestra containing two violins, a piano, a double bass, and two bandoneons. (A bandoneon is similar to a small accordion.)

Today, many countries have created their own style of tango dancing. Each year, Buenos Aires hosts the Tango World Championships, which attract hundreds of dancers from countries around the world.

Tango is an elegant and dramatic dance.

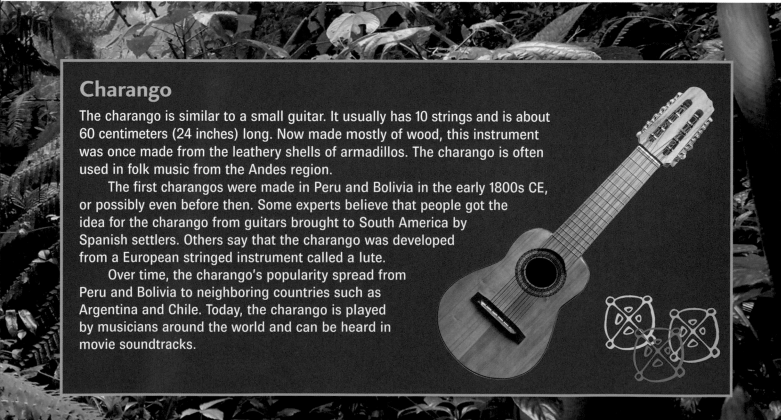

Charango

The charango is similar to a small guitar. It usually has 10 strings and is about 60 centimeters (24 inches) long. Now made mostly of wood, this instrument was once made from the leathery shells of armadillos. The charango is often used in folk music from the Andes region.

The first charangos were made in Peru and Bolivia in the early 1800s CE, or possibly even before then. Some experts believe that people got the idea for the charango from guitars brought to South America by Spanish settlers. Others say that the charango was developed from a European stringed instrument called a lute.

Over time, the charango's popularity spread from Peru and Bolivia to neighboring countries such as Argentina and Chile. Today, the charango is played by musicians around the world and can be heard in movie soundtracks.

Ocarina

The Maya of Mexico and Central America played a small flute-like clay instrument called the ocarina. This instrument has several finger holes, which can be covered to produce different notes. There is also a hole the performer blows into to create sound. The Maya, and later the Aztecs, often made ocarinas in the shape of an animal or bird. Some evidence suggests that other cultures in Latin America made an instrument similar to the ocarina, in some cases as early as 2000 BCE.

Modern ocarinas may be made of clay, metal, wood, or plastic. There is even ocarina software that works with cell phones and tablet computers. The user blows into the microphone and covers finger holes that appear on the screen to produce the sounds of an ocarina.

A Peruvian man plays the zampoña.

A traditional clay ocarina

Zampoña

Many cultures around the world use an ancient wind instrument called the pan flute, which is a set of narrow tubes cut at different lengths and played by blowing across the tops of the tubes. Hundreds of years ago, South Americans developed their own version of the pan flute, called the *zampoña* (pronounced *sahm-pone-ya*). This instrument is made from the thick reeds of plants such as bamboo.

The zampoña (sometimes called a siku or antara) is played in the Andes regions of Peru, Ecuador, Colombia, Bolivia, Chile, and Argentina.

Maracas

Maracas are made from dried gourds or coconut shells filled with seeds or beans, with a handle attached. They are almost always played two at a time. Traditionally, maracas have been popular in many Latin American countries, such as Cuba and Colombia, as well as in Puerto Rico.

Today, maracas are featured in a wide variety of music, from traditional Latin music to pop and rock and roll. Modern maracas come in many different sizes and are often made from plastic or wood.

Traditional maracas made from gourds

MUSIC AND DANCE *continued*

Mariachi

It's hard to miss mariachi music in Mexico, especially at festivals or in city squares. Mariachi bands are a part of Mexican culture that is famous around the world. They are easy to recognize because of their matching decorated outfits and large sombrero hats. The musicians' instruments may vary, but usually include violins, trumpets, a guitar, and a guitarron (an extra-large guitar). Mariachi bands often play at weddings and other celebrations, and can be heard outside Mexico anywhere there is a large Mexican community.

This mariachi band features a guitarron (center).

Salsa

You may have heard of salsa as a type of food, but did you know that it is also a style of music and dance? Salsa music mixes together several different styles of Latin music, most of which come from Cuba. About 50 years ago, Cubans and Puerto Ricans brought salsa to New York City and it is now popular around the world.

Salsa bands use lots of percussion instruments, especially the cowbell. Other instruments include the trumpet, trombone, and guitar. In the salsa dance, couples combine basic steps with hip movements and twirls.

A Cuban couple dances the salsa.

Chinchineros

Chinchinero is the name for a one-man band from Chile. A chinchinero is a street performer, usually a man or a boy, who carries a drum on his back and plays it by using long drumsticks. A rope connects cymbals on top of the drum to the chinchinero's feet. By moving his feet, the chinchinero makes the cymbals crash together.

Chinchineros often combine their music with a dance that involves quick steps and spinning in circles.

The chinchinero tradition started in Chile about 50 years ago, and now the musicians can be seen playing in streets and city squares around the country.

Two young chinchineros in Santiago, Chile

A Chilean cowboy and his partner dance the cueca.

Cueca

Cueca is a dance over 200 years old that is performed in Chile, Peru, Bolivia, and some parts of Argentina. The dance is said to imitate a rooster courting a hen. During the dance, couples wave handkerchiefs in the air while they circle around each other.

Cueca is also the name of the style of music played for the dance, though in some regions of Latin America this musical style is known as "La Chilena."

In Chile, where cueca is the official national dance, cueca is performed during the country's Independence Day celebrations. The typical cueca costume in Chile includes a dress for the woman, and a poncho, boots, and a type of rancher hat for the man.

SPORTS

Several unique sports have developed in Latin America. Some of these sports, such as rodeo and capoeira, are now popular around the world.

Tinku

In the Andes mountains of Bolivia, men have been meeting once a year for hundreds of years to fist fight. The ritual is called *tinku*, which means "encounter" or "attack" in the local languages. The sport can sometimes be dangerous, but locals say it is a way to release tension, which helps reduce violent outbursts for the rest of the year. Today, the ritual is more often performed as a dance, with dancers wearing colorful clothing as they move to the warlike beat of a drum.

Tinku dancers at a Bolivian festival in Chile

Capoeira

Capoeira (pronounced *cap-uh-ware-ah*) is a sport that combines dance and martial arts. It was invented in Brazil about 400 years ago, most likely by slaves brought from Africa. The slaves disguised martial arts training as dance so their owners wouldn't forbid it. After the end of slavery in the late 1800s, capoeira was declared illegal, though over time it was accepted in Brazilian society and developed into the artistic sport popular today.

To play capoeira, one or two participants (called *capoeiristas*) stand inside of a circle of people who sing, clap, and play musical instruments. The people inside the circle make attack and defense movements, using kicks, flips, and cartwheels. Today, the sport is taught and performed around the world.

Brazilian capoeiristas demonstrate their skill.

Futsal

Invented in Uruguay in 1930 CE, futsal was a less expensive form of soccer for young people. This sport is played on a court (usually indoors), with five players per team and a smaller ball and shorter games than soccer. Futsal spread to Brazil, where some of that country's most famous soccer players got their start by playing futsal. The sport spread from South America to Europe, the United States, and Canada. Today, there are more than 2 million futsal players around the world.

A player from Brazil (in yellow) competes in the 2008 FIFA Futsal World Cup.

Lucha Libre

This dramatic style of wrestling started in Mexico in the early 1900s CE. It involves two wrestlers (called *luchadores*), who perform not only wrestling but also high-flying, acrobatic moves inside the ring. This sport is also known for the colorful masks worn by the wrestlers. The term *lucha libre* is Spanish for "free fighting." Now one of the most popular sports in Mexico, lucha libre also has fans in the United States and Japan.

Rodeo

In the 1800s CE, cowboys in the most northern provinces of Mexico (these provinces later became part of the southwestern United States) turned the daily activities of cattle ranching into the sporting event that we know as a rodeo. Participants compete at such things as being the fastest to lasso and tie up a calf, and riding a bucking bull for as long as possible before falling off.

Rodeos became popular throughout South America, including in Brazil, where one of the world's largest annual rodeos takes place. Mexico has its own version of the rodeo, called a *charreada*. Rodeos are also popular in the United States and Canada, where dozens are held each year.

A Mexican charreada

LATIN AMERICA TODAY

More than ever before, people around the world are paying attention to Latin America. Its industries are growing quickly, and many Latin Americans—from writers to athletes to pop stars—have achieved worldwide fame.

Mexico City, Mexico

The Cathedral of Brasilia in Brazil was designed by Oscar Niemeyer.

Booming Cities

Although many Latin Americans live in small rural villages, some of the world's biggest cities are found in Latin America. Mexico City (in Mexico), São Paulo (in Brazil), and Buenos Aires (in Argentina) each have a population of over 10 million. Some cities are known for their architecture, which may include beautiful old museums and cathedrals, as well as spectacular modern buildings. Cultural events, such as large theater and music festivals, are popular in many Latin American cities.

Michelle Bachelet

Democracy

Democracy is a political system in which people vote to choose their local and national leaders. Many Latin American countries have strong democracies where people express their opinions by voting on election day. Women often play an active role in Latin American politics—for example, Michelle Bachelet was president of Chile from 2006 to 2010, and Dilma Rousseff became president of Brazil in 2011.

Preserving Traditional Cultures

Many traditional cultures still exist in Latin America. These cultures are valued as an important part of Latin America's heritage, and many of them have fought hard to keep their language and traditions from dying out. Bolivian president Evo Morales (whose heritage is the Aymara people of Bolivia, Chile, and Peru) has supported efforts in his country to preserve traditional languages.

The Maya in Central America today are descendants of the ancient Maya. The Mapuche culture of southern Chile has existed since long before the time of the Incas. South America is one of the few places left on earth where people of some ancient cultures still live their traditional lifestyles without any contact with people from the "modern world."

Evo Morales

Many tourists enjoy hiking in the mountains.

Tourism

It's no wonder tourists love to visit Latin American countries—they are home to some of the most fascinating places on earth. The warm weather and beautiful beaches of countries such as Cuba, the Dominican Republic, Mexico, and Brazil make these popular destinations for visitors.

For tourists who want a more adventurous vacation, there are many options: hiking along the ancient Inca Trail in Peru, skiing or mountain climbing in the Andes, and exploring the jungles of Central America, just to name a few.

The magnificent Iguazu Falls on the border of Argentina and Brazil are a sight that visitors to the area don't want to miss.

The Iguazu Falls

Natural Resources

Harvesting sugar cane in Cuba

Since European explorers began to search for gold and silver in Latin America hundreds of years ago, people from around the world have continued the search for valuable natural resources. Mining and other industries, such as logging and agriculture, are very important in many Latin American countries. These industries produce products that are sold around the world.

Chile is the world's largest producer of copper, while Mexico and Peru are leaders in silver production. Brazil is the world's largest exporter of ethanol, a fuel made from plants.

Some industries in Latin America continue to work hard to find ways to avoid harming the environment.

The Arts

Throughout its history, Latin America has produced great artists such as Diego Rivera (see page 21), as well as many writers and poets who have become famous around the world. The Nobel Prize for Literature is the top literary award in the world, and Latin Americans have won this prize several times. Past winners include Gabriela Mistral (Chile), Miguel Ángel Asturias (Guatemala), Pablo Neruda (Chile), Gabriel García Márquez (Colombia), and Octavio Paz (Mexico).

Latin Americans have also made their mark in the world of pop music, bringing the rhythms of "Latin dance pop" to a worldwide audience. The Colombian singer and songwriter Shakira has won many awards for her songs. Ricky Martin, from Puerto Rico, became an international star after releasing the song "Livin' la Vida Loca," which is written in a style similar to salsa. (See page 34 for more information on salsa music and dance.)

Pop star Ricky Martin

Sports

Soccer is one sport that Latin Americans are crazy about and also very good at. In Latin America, this sport is called *fútbol* (Spanish) or *futebol* (Portuguese). Most players start as children and some go on to play in professional leagues. Teams from Brazil and Argentina have won the World Cup several times, and many other Latin American countries have strong teams, including Mexico and Uruguay.

Athletes from Latin America have become well known for their skill in other sports, including baseball players from the Dominican Republic, Puerto Rico, and Venezuela; basketball players from Brazil; and tennis players from Argentina.

Surfing is quickly becoming a popular sport in countries such as Ecuador, Panama, Brazil, Peru, and Chile. Surfers seek out the best spots along the coast for catching the big waves.

Professional Puerto Rican surfer Idalis "Lilac" Alvarado

A BRIEF TIMELINE OF LATIN AMERICA

An Olmec stone mask

Before 1492 (Pre-Columbian Era)

Many ancient cultures develop and thrive for thousands of years. The Olmecs live in Central America around 1000 BCE, and are followed by the Maya civilization. The Maya build many great cities between 250 BCE and 1250 CE. Meanwhile, millions of people belonging to many different cultures build communities throughout Latin America, including the Moche in Peru, the Aymara in Bolivia, and various groups in the Amazon. In the later years, around 1400 CE, the Aztecs in Mexico become a powerful group. Around the same time, the Incas build their empire in Peru.

European explorer Christopher Columbus

1492–1810 (Colonial Era)

European explorers arrive in Latin America, bringing useful animals but also deadly diseases. The explorers force the local people to speak European languages and follow the Catholic religion. They also make many people work as slaves. Some communities fight back, while others cooperate with the Europeans. Many new cities and towns are built across Latin America. People begin to make greater use of natural resources, including mining for gold, silver, and copper.

The Panama Canal

1810–Present (Independence)

After a long struggle, Latin American countries gain independence from Europe. Many different governments rule individual countries, sometimes taking control by military force. In 1914, the Panama Canal opens in Central America, making global trade by ships much easier. National governments from inside and outside Latin America, as well as other groups, fight over natural resources. Eventually, most countries adopt a democratic system, in which citizens vote for their national leader.

Further Reading

DK Publishing. *Aztec, Inca & Maya* (DK Eyewitness Books series). New York: DK Publishing, 2011.

Gruber, Beth. *Mexico* (National Geographic Countries of the World series). Washington, DC: National Geographic Society, 2009.

Richardson, Hazel. *Life in Ancient South America* (Peoples in the Ancient World series). New York: Crabtree, 2005.

Turck, Mary C. *Mexico and Central America: A Fiesta of Cultures, Crafts, and Activities for Ages 8–12.* Chicago: Chicago Review Press, 2004.

Woods, Michael, and Woods, Mary B. *Seven Natural Wonders of Central and South America.* Minneapolis, MN: Twenty-First Century Books, 2009.

Wright, David K. *Cuba: Enchantment of the World.* Chicago: Children's Press, 2008.

Selected Sources

Campos Muñoz, Luis. *Relaciones Interétnicas: En Pueblos Originarios de México y Chile.* Santiago: Universidad Academia de Humanismo Cristiano, 2008.

Crosby, Alfred W. *The Columbian Exchange: Biological and Cultural Consequences of 1492*, 30th anniversary ed. Westport, CT: Praeger Publishers, 2003.

D'Altroy, Terence N. *The Incas.* Oxford, UK: Blackwell Publishing, 2003.

Fernandez-Armesto, Felipe. *The Americas: A Hemispheric History.* New York: Modern Library, 2005.

Morris, Walter F., Jr. *Living Maya.* New York: Harry N. Abrams, 2000.

Reid, Michael. *Forgotten Continent: The Battle for Latin America's Soul.* New Haven and London: Yale University Press, 2009.

Williamson, Edwin. *The Penguin History of Latin America.* London and New York: Penguin Books, 2009.

Winn, Peter. *Americas: The Changing Face of Latin America and the Caribbean.* Berkeley, Los Angeles, and London: University of California Press, 2006.

Credits

Cover main, © Jeromaniac; **cover bottom right,** © Lunamarina; **3,** © Dmitry Rukhlenko; **5 bottom right,** © Kavalles; **5 top left,** © Lisavan; **5 middle left,** © Luis Fernandez; **6–7 top, back cover minor background,** © Quoc Anh Lai; **7 background,** © Lorpic99; **7 foreground,** © Ben Goode; **8 top left,** © Martin Battiti; **8 second left,** © Hotshotsworldwide; **8 third left,** © Hxdbzxy; **8 fourth left,** © Dirk Ercken; **8 right,** © Edurivero; **9 right,** © Suljo; **12 middle left,** © Dmitry Rukhlenko; **13 background,** © Nico Smit; **13 clockwise from top far left:** © Edyta Pawlowska; © Uros Ravbar; © Davthy; © Mirmoor; **15 top,** © Steve Allen; **15 bottom,** © Velvetweb; **15 background,** © Jarnogz; **16 bottom,** © Mirmoor; **16–17 background,** © Emma Rogers; **17 top,** © Jarnogz; **17 bottom,** © Bernardo Ertl; **18 background, 19 background,** both © Bernadette Lopez; **19 bottom,** © Shargaljut; **20 top,** © Maria Teresa Weinmann; **21 bottom,** © Bevanward; **21 background,** © Jorgeinthe; **22 top right,** © Luis Fernandez; **22 background,** © Patricia Marroquin; **23 bottom left,** © Tamara Bauer; **24 bottom,** © Todd Taulman; **24 background,** © Spectral-design; **25 bottom right,** © Bevanward; **25 bottom left,** © Aleksandr Lobanov; **27 top,** © Norman Chan; **27 left,** © Antonio Oquias; **27 background,** © Pierre-yves Babelon; **28 top first,** © Lightzoom; **28 top second,** © Tomboy2290; **28 top third,** © Ildipapp; **28 bottom left,** © Magdalena Żurawska; **28 bottom right,** © Robert Kneschke; **28 background,** © Lee Torrens; **29 top main,** © Gabrieldome; **29 top inset,** © Danelle Mccollum; **29 middle,** © Álvaro Germán Vilela; **29 background,** © Slavenko Vukasovic; **29 bottom first,** © Riley Maclean; **29 bottom second,** © Artography; **29 bottom third,** © Eyewave; **30 right,** © Glenda Powers; **30 bottom inset,** © Jesús Eloy Ramos Lara; **31 top right,** © Ariwasabi; **32 top,** © Andrii Deviatov; **32 bottom,** © Sergii Shcherbakov; **33 top right,** © Tln; **33 bottom, back cover third,** © Mark Fairey; **34 background,** © Oscar1319; **37 background, 47 background,** both © King Ho Yim; **38 top,** © Hector Fernandez; **39 bottom,** © Simon Wedege Petersen; **39 background,** © Paop; **40 top,** © Galyna Andrushko; **40 bottom,** © Richard Semik; **40 background,** © Tomasz Pado; **41 bottom,** © Eric Rivera; **41 background,** © Andreas Jancso; **42 top,** © Leon Rafael; **42 bottom, back cover major background,** © Yanik Chauvin: all © Dreamstime.com. **Cover top right, 18 bottom,** courtesy Chez Cåsver; **18 top, back cover first,** courtesy Kwamikagami; **27 right,** courtesy Tom White: all http://commons.wikimedia.org/wiki. **23 top right,** © British Museum/Eileen Tweedy; **14 bottom,** © Museo Ciudad, Mexico/Collection Dagli Orti; **21 top,** © National Palace, Mexico City/Gianni Dagli Orti: image D.R. © 2011 Banco de México, "Fiduciario" en el Fideicomiso relativo a los Museos Diego Rivera y Frida Kahlo. Av. Cinco de Mayo No. 2, Col. Centro, Del. Cuauhtémoc 06059, México, D.F.; **22 top left,** Museo Banco Central de Quito, Ecuador/Gianni Dagli Orti; **cover bottom left, 23 top left,** Archaeological Museum, Lima/Gianni Dagli Orti: all © The Art Archive. **5 top right,** © Matt Tilghman; **5 bottom left, 12 top,** © Doug Von Gausig; **8 background, 32 background, 42 background,** © Francisco Romero; **13 bottom left, back cover second,** © Bartosz Hadyniak; **14 top,** ©`Dawn Nichols; **16 top,** © Maria Veras; **25 background,** © Maria Pavlova; **25 top right,** © Niko Guido; **25 top left,** © traveler1116; **30 left,** © DNY59; **31 bottom,** © Gema Blanton; **33 top left,** © Bartosz Hadyniak; **34 top,** © Cristian Lazzari; **34 bottom, back cover bottom,** Niko Guido; **38 bottom,** King Ho Yim; **42 middle,** Constance McGuire: all © iStockphoto, Inc. **6 bottom, 47,** both © Christian Peña Photography. **9 top left,** *Codex Borbonicus*, Paris, 1899: courtesy Beinecke Rare Book and Manuscript Library, Yale University. **9 bottom left,** © Kike Calvo via AP Images; **37 top,** AP Photo/Ricardo Moraes. **12 middle right,** © peter jordan; **19 top,** © Mireille Vautier; **22 bottom,** © A. Robert Turner; **24 top,** © Edward Parker; **26 top left,** © imagebroker; **30 main bottom,** © David Young-Wolff; **31 left,** © nobleIMAGES; **35 bottom,** © Picture Contact BV; **36 bottom,** © David Muenker; **37 middle,** © Chico anchez/Aurora Photos; **37 bottom,** © Karina Tkach; **39 top,** © ITAR-TASS Photo Agency; **41 top,** © United Archives GmbH: all © Alamy. **12 bottom left,** Library of Congress Prints and Photographs Division, reproduction number: LC-USZ62-56643. **12 bottom right,** © CraterValley Photo - Fotolia.com. **13 bottom right,** © Tim Draper; **26 right,** © Steve Gorton: both © Dorling Kindersley. **20 bottom,** Museum of Anthropology, University of Missouri. **26 bottom left, 36 top,** both © Eva Salinas. **28 top fourth,** courtesy United States Department of Agriculture. **35 top,** © Pablo Corral V/CORBIS.

Index

A
aji peppers, 28
alpaca, 13
Andes Mountains, 7, 13, 26, 27
Argentina
    Buenos Aires, city of, 32, 38
    charango (guitar), 32
    cueca (dance), 35
    mate (drink), 28
    poncho, 13
    soccer, 41
    tango, 32
    zampoña (flute), 33
Asturias, Miguel Ángel, 41
Aymara peoples, 39, 42
Aztec peoples
    cacao beans, 27
    calendar systems of, 18
    chewing gum, 24
    chocolate, 27
    ocarina (musical instrument), 33
    piñata, 30
    timeline of, 42
    tomatoes, 28

B
Bachelet, Michelle, 39
baseball, 41
basketball, 41
Belize, 13, 17
    Mayan cities, 17
bell peppers, 28
Bolivia
    charango (guitar), 32
    chili peppers, 28
    cueca (dance), 35
    farming, 14
    mate (drink), 28
    mining in, 15
    raised fields (chinampas), 14
    tinku (sport), 36
    zampoña (flute), 33
Bonampak, Mexico, 20
Brazil
    cacao beans, 27
    capoeira, 36
    Carnival, 31
    futsal, 37
    mate (drink), 28
    Rio de Janeiro, city of, 31
    rodeo, 37
    Rousseff, Dilma, 39
    São Paulo, city of, 38
    soccer, 41
    tourism in, 40
Buenos Aires, Argentina, 32, 38

C
cacao beans, 27
calendar systems, ancient, 18
capoeira (sport), 36
carnivals, 31
cascarones (celebration eggs), 22
champurrado (drink), 27
charango (guitar), 32
charreada (rodeo), 37
chasqui (messenger), 19
chewing gum, production of, 24
Chile, 17
    Bachelet, Michelle, 39
    building for earthquakes, 17
    charango (guitar), 32
    chinchinero (musician), 35
    cueca (dance), 35
    food, 26
    mate (drink), 28
    Mistral, Gabriela, 41
    Neruda, Pablo, 41
    poncho, 13
    Santiago, city of, 6, 7
    zampoña (flute), 33
chili peppers, 28
chinampas (raised fields), 14
chinchinero (musician), 35
chocolate, 27
cities, modern Latin American, 38
cocoa beans
    see cacao beans
Colombia
    maracas (musical instrument), 33
    Márquez, Gabriel García, 41
    Shakira, 9, 41
    zampoña (flute), 33
Colonial era, 42
Columbus, Christopher, 8, 25, 31
Cuba
    dulce de leche, 29
    maracas (musical instrument), 33
    quinceañera celebration, 31
    salsa (music), 34
    tobacco, 25
    tourism in, 40
cueca (dance), 35
curanto (hot stones), 26

D
Day of the Dead (*Dia de los Muertos*), 30
Day of the Race (*Dia de la Raza*), 31
definition, Latin America, 7–9
democracy, in Latin America, 39, 42
de Santa Anna, General Antonio Lopez, 24
Dia de la Raza (Day of the Race) celebration, 31

Dia de los Muertos (Day of the Dead) celebration, 30
Dominican Republic
    baseball, 41
    dulce de leche, 29
    tourism in, 40
dulce de leche, 29

E
earthquakes, building for, 17
Ecuador
    masks, 22
    Panama hat, 12
    sombrero de paja toquilla (hat), 12
    zampoña (flute), 33
El Salvador
    huipil (blouse), 13
    Mayan cities, 17
Eye of God (Ojo de Dios), 23

F
fields, raised (chinampas), 14
FIFA World Cup, 37, 41
freeze-dried food, 26
fútbol (soccer), 41
futebol (soccer, Portuguese), 41
futsal (sport), 37

G
gourd carvings, 20
guanaco, 13
Guarani peoples, 28
Guatemala, 17
    Asturias, Miguel Ángel, 41
    gourd carvings, 20
    huipil (blouse), 13
    Mayan cities, 17
    worry dolls, 25

H
hammocks, invention of, 24
hieroglyphs, Mayan, 18
history, Latin America, 42
Honduras, 17
    Mayan cities, 17
Huichol peoples, 23
huipil (blouse), 13

I
Iguazu Falls, 40
Inca peoples
    chasqui (messenger), 19
    irrigation system, farmland, 14
    Machu Picchu, 16, 27
    metal work of, 21
    mit'a (tax system), 15
    pottery of, 23
    quipu (communication system), 19

stonework of, 17
timeline of, 42
Independence era, 42
irrigation system, farmland, 14
irrigation systems, 14

J
jalapeño peppers, 28

L
labor tax, 15
Lent, 31
llama, 13
lucha libre, 37

M
Machu Picchu, 16, 27
maize, 29
maps, Latin America, 10–11
Mapuche peoples, 13, 29, 39
maracas (musical instrument), 33
mariachi band, 34
Márquez, Gabriel García, 41
Martin, Ricky, 41
masks, 22
mate (drink), 28
Mayan peoples
    cacao beans, 27
    calendar systems of, 18
    chewing gum, 24
    clothing design, 13
    hieroglyphs of, 18
    huipil (blouse), 13
    murals of, 20
    ocarina (musical instrument), 33
    piñata, 30
    pottery of, 23
    pyramids of, 17
    timeline of, 42
metal work, 21
Mexico, 17
    Bonampak murals, 20
    cacao beans, 27
    cascarones (celebration eggs), 22
    champurrado (drink), 27
    chili peppers, 28
    Diego Rivera, 41
    farming, 14
    lucha libre, 37
    mariachi band, 34
    Mayan cities, 17
    murals, modern, 21
    Ojo de Dios (Eye of God), 23
    Paz, Octavio, 41
    quinceañera celebration, 31
    raised fields (chinampas), 14
    Rivera, Diego, 21
    rodeo, 37
    soccer, 41
    sombrero (hat), 12
    tourism in, 40
Mexico City, Mexico, 14, 38

Mistral, Gabriela, 41
mit'a (tax system), 15
Moche peoples, 42
Morales, President Evo, 39
mountain farming, 27
murals
    Mayan, 20
    modern, 21

N
natural resources, Latin American,
    40, 42
Neruda, Pablo, 41
Niemeyer, Oscar, 38
Nobel Prize for Literature, 41

O
ocarina (musical instrument), 33
Ojo de Dios (Eye of God), 23
Olmec peoples, 22, 25, 27, 42

P
Panama Canal, 42
Panama hat, 12
Paraguay
    mate (drink), 28
Paz, Octavio, 41
peanuts, 29
Peru
    charango (guitar), 32
    chili peppers, 28
    cueca (dance), 35
    gourd carvings, 20
    irrigation system, farmland, 14
    Machu Picchu, 16, 27
    potatoes, 29
    pottery of, 23
    salt mines in, 15
    zampoña (flute), 33
piñata, 30
politics
    democracy, 39
poncho, 13
potatoes, 29
pottery, 23
Pre-Columbian era, 42
Puerto Rico
    baseball, 41
    maracas (musical instrument), 33
    Martin, Ricky, 41
    masks, 22
    quinceañera celebration, 31
    salsa (music), 34
pyramids, Mayan, 17

Q
quinceañera celebration, 31
quipu (communication system), 19

R
Rio de Janeiro, Brazil, 31
Rivera, Diego, 21, 41

rodeo, 37
Roosevelt, President Theodore, 12
Rousseff, Dilma, 39
rubber production, 25

S
salsa (food), 28
salsa (music), 34
Santiago, Chile, 6, 7
São Paulo, Brazil, 38
Shakira, 9, 41
soccer, 41
sombrero de paja toquilla (hat), 12
sombrero (hat), 12
Spanish explorers, 21, 27, 29, 42
stonework, Inca, 17
Stuart, David, 18
sugar cane, 41
"Sun Stone," 18
surfing, 41

T
tabasco peppers, 28
Taino peoples, 24
tango (dance), 32
tennis, 41
Tenochtitlan, city of, 14
terrace farming, 27
timeline of Latin America, 42
tinku (ritual sport), 36
tobacco, 25
tomatoes, 28
tourism, in Latin America, 40
traditional cultures, in Latin American

U
Uruguay
    futsal (sport), 37
    mate (drink), 28
    soccer, 41
    tango (dance), 32

V
vanilla beans, 29
Venezuela, 41
vicuña, 13

W
wildlife, 8
wool, 13
World Cup, soccer, 41
worry dolls, 25
wrestling (lucha libre), 37

Z
zampoña (flute), 33

EVA SALINAS was born in Sault Ste. Marie, Ontario. She later moved to Toronto, Ontario, where she received her Bachelor of Journalism degree from Ryerson University.

Eva briefly lived in London, England, where she worked with the Wandsworth Prison media project, which trains inmates to produce radio broadcasts. She later lived in Vancouver, British Columbia, working as a reporter for *The Globe and Mail*, and in Accra, Ghana, as a trainer for the organization Journalists for Human Rights.

Returning to Toronto, Eva worked for *The National Post*, *This Magazine*, and Athletes for Africa, which provides support to African youth affected by war. She then realized a lifelong dream of exploring her Latin American roots when she headed south for Chile. Based in Santiago, Eva worked as the editor of *The Santiago Times*, where she covered, among other things, Sebastián Piñera's 2010 election as president, the 8.8-magnitude earthquake, and the rescue of the 33 miners in the Atacama Desert.

Eva is based in Toronto, where she remains passionate about Latin America, human rights, and arts and culture.

Also in Annick's acclaimed **We Thought of It** series:

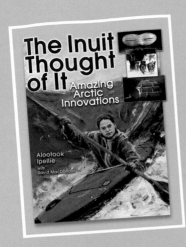

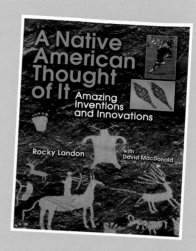

★ "The Year's Best" List, *Resource Links*
★ Children's "Non-Fiction Top 10" List,
  Ontario Library Association
★ Best Books for Kids & Teens 2008, starred selection,
  Canadian Children's Book Centre
★ 2008 Skipping Stones Honor Award
★ 2009 Silver Birch Award nomination

"Chock-a-block full of interesting information
and pictures." —*CM Magazine*

"[An] informative and easy to read book … attractive
and useful." —*Children's Book News*

★ Best Books for Kids & Teens 2009, Canadian
  Children's Book Centre
★ "The Year's Best" List, *Resource Links*
★ 2010/2011 Red Cedar Book Award nomination

"Deserves a permanent spot on any
reader's bookshelf." —*ForeWord Reviews*

"A real eye-opener to enlighten children and
adults alike." —*Resource Links*

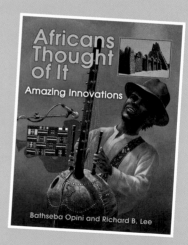

★ "Best Bets" List, Ontario Library Association
★ 2010 Best Books, Canadian Children's Book Centre

"A well-focused introduction to the history of
technological innovation in China."
—*Booklist Online*

"An informative and entertaining read."
—*ForeWord Reviews*

★ 2011 Skipping Stones Honor Book

"This book is a wealth of information for anyone
studying about African countries and their cultures."
—*CM Magazine*

"No matter how much you know about the traditions
and products of this vast multi-cultural continent,
[this] will reveal something new."
—*ForeWord Reviews*

Go to www.annickpress.com to view book trailers for these and other exciting titles.

DISCARD

J 980 SALINAS

Salinas, Eva.
Latin Americans
thought of it

METRO

R4002050043

METROPOLITAN
Atlanta-Fulton Public Library